Dearest Samantha: I Love You!!!!

Stories of Hope and Encouragement
for Hurting Women

Heather L. Smith

WESTBOW
PRESS
A DIVISION OF THOMAS NELSON

WestBow Press books may be ordered through booksellers or by contacting:

WestBow Press
A Division of Thomas Nelson
1663 Liberty Drive
Bloomington, IN 47403
www.westbowpress.com
1-(866) 928-1240

ISBN: 978-1-4497-6056-4 (sc)
ISBN: 978-1-4497-6055-7 (e)

Library of Congress Control Number: 2012912992

Printed in the United States of America

WestBow Press rev. date: 08/30/2012

To
David and Marcia, Sharon and Lee—
my precious children and their dear spouses.
Cory, Samantha, Tabitha, and Jimmy—
my beloved grandchildren.
Oliver H. Lee, Jr. and Julia C. Lee—
my cherished parents.
All my love.

CONTENTS

PREFACE

This little book of stories was written just for you, my friend. They were written following the birth of my granddaughter, Samantha, during my months in the wilderness.

The stories are true and have been breathed on by Him who shares your pain and understands the hurt and grief you experience. Inspired by the Holy Spirit, these stories are a reflection of the precious love the Lord Jesus Christ has for *you*.

Beloved, Samantha is you, my dear. She is you: discouraged, lonely, and brokenhearted. She is you: struggling so hard and feeling no one cares. Finally, she is you: about to give up because the pain is too much to bear.

My prayer is that the stories will comfort you and give you hope for there is One who has gone before you and has walked in your shoes.

He longs to comfort you with His sweet words of love.

He yearns to embrace you with His strong arms of compassion.

He desires to kiss you and always wipe all of your tears.

He wants to take you away with Him and change your heart forever.

My friend, Jesus loves you so very much.

You are His beloved—His bride.

Go to Him; He is waiting for you.

May God richly bless you, my dear, and may you "grasp how wide and long and high and deep is the love of Christ, and to know this love that surpasses knowledge—that you may be filled to the measure of all the fullness of God" (Ephesians 3:18-19).

Please know I will be lifting you and your loved ones up each day to the Father. I love you!

Unless otherwise noted, all Scripture references in this book are taken from the Holy Bible New International Version®. NIV®. Copyright © 1973, 1978, 1984, 2011 by Biblica.

CHAPTER 1

—ɱ—

INTRODUCTION

Let him lead me to the banquet hall, and let his banner over me be love.

— Song of Solomon 2:4

D early Beloved:

You are a beautiful and talented person. As promised in the verse from Song of Solomon, God has a wonderful plan for your life. He made you special and gifted with extraordinary talents. His unique plan for your life will give you deep purpose and meaning.

There is only one of you, my dear. When God created you, He designed a magnificent work for you alone. If you do not know His plan for your life, ask the Father to show you.

Several years ago, my marriage ended, and I subsequently lost my home. My husband and I were married almost thirty years. The walk through the wilderness has been difficult. For a while I did not think I would make it. However, through the sorrow and grief, the Father has been with me. You see, my friend, we are not alone, for there is One who loves us more than life itself—the Lord Jesus Christ, who gave up His life for us.

In this difficult world we live in "he will never leave you nor forsake you" (Deuteronomy 31:6). In the blackest of nights, alone in my little house in the woods, He has comforted me and given me His peace. And in the midst of the hurt, God has been faithful and provided for my every need. The Father has given me vision to touch the lives of hurting people with His unfailing love through sharing my testimony and praying for others.

Dear friend, *you* are so precious to Him. You are His most cherished creation. If you do not know Christ, my sister, please give Him a chance and ask Him into your heart; you will never be sorry for taking this step of faith.

For Jesus will take away *all* of your sorrows and disappointments and replace them with indescribable joy! I know because He did it for me. God bless you, my friend.

I love you!
Heather

CHAPTER 2

—ෲ—

LONELINESS

You, LORD, are my lamp; the LORD turns my darkness
into light.

— 2 Samuel 22:29

D early Beloved:

Several years ago I lost my home; God moved me
into a house in the woods for a time of healing. My little rented
house was approximately twenty-five miles from work. Often,
it would be dark before I got home.

One of my neighbors had a beautiful yard with a split-rail
fence at the edge of his property. Electric lights were installed
on each post. Many times when I drove by, the lights would
twinkle in the darkness. They comforted me and reminded me
God was near.

On the way home one night, I felt a substantive loneliness
weigh upon me. I said aloud as I drove, "Oh, Lord, if You loved
me, the lights would be on." I had not seen the lamps lit in some

time and felt the chances of the lights being on that particular night were slim.

God hears our prayers, dear friend. When I drove down the hill toward home, long before I got to my neighbor's house, the lights were shining brightly in the darkness!

A few weeks later one Friday night, driving home I told the Father, "Oh, Lord, I can't wait to get home to be with You." As I drove toward my neighbor's house, much to my joy, the lights were on again. It was as if He was saying, "Heather, I can't wait to be with you, too!"

Dear friend, the Father loves you so much. He will light your way in the darkness.

I love you!
Heather

CHAPTER 3

—∞—

DIAMONDS

I took you from the ends of the earth, from its farthest corners I called you. I said, 'You are my servant'; I have chosen you and have not rejected you. So do not fear, for I am with you; do not be dismayed, for I am your God. I will strengthen you and help you; I will uphold you with my righteous right hand.

— Isaiah 41:9-10

Dearly Beloved:

Several years ago, we had a bad winter. Hardly would one storm pass through, leaving its aftermath of ice and snow, when another blizzard would move in to take its place. It was a time during which God taught me how to live by faith.

One Saturday night, a major snowstorm was en route to my area. I knelt and asked the Lord to spare us. It was during a critical time at work; it was imperative for me to be there each day. The storm passed over and all we experienced were a few flakes!

God hears our prayers, dear friend. When the roads became impassable during the hard winter and I could not reach home, He provided me with safe, inexpensive places to stay. When a large tree fell on my house and tore up the roof, I did not have renter's insurance. However, no snow or ice came through the ceiling to damage my things.

I lived at the bottom of a hill. My car was parked at the hilltop. For weeks, the hill was covered with a sheet of ice. During this time, I learned to depend totally on the Father. Twice a day, I faced the hill, but God was right beside me and kept my feet from falling on the treacherous slope.

Many times during that harsh winter, I had to leave my car at the end of the long driveway to slip and slide my way to the little house in the woods. My thoughtful landlord always left a light on outside to help me find my way through the black night.

The snow and ice looked like a shimmering blanket embedded with diamonds brilliantly shining in the darkness. The effect was breathtaking!

After that difficult winter, I began to see diamonds in the most ordinary places. Look closely, my friend, at the interstate blacktop. Can't you see diamonds sparkling in the concrete?

One night I was in church praying; I had grieved the Lord that day. Even though I had asked for His forgiveness, I could not get rid of my guilty feelings. I asked God to take away my condemning thoughts and touch my heart with His love.

As I was praying, I opened my eyes and looked up. I was beside the concrete wall in the sanctuary. Embedded in the cement were tiny chips sparkling like diamonds.

My precious friend, in this dark world, you are His diamond. You are to shine like stars in the universe "as you hold firmly to the word of life" (Philippians 2:16).

Keep looking to Jesus, my dear. He is polishing you to shine for Him.

I love you!
Heather

CHAPTER 4

—⚭—

GRIEF

The LORD is close to the brokenhearted and saves those who are crushed in spirit.

— Psalm 34:18

The LORD your God is with you, the Mighty Warrior who saves. He will take great delight in you; in his love he will no longer rebuke you, but will rejoice over you with singing.

— Zephaniah 3:17

Dearly Beloved:

Just a note to let you know, my dear friend, I am thinking about you and lifting you up to our loving heavenly Father. I know times may be difficult for you now. The Lord understands so well the hurt and pain you are experiencing. I am praying God will comfort and sustain you with His unfailing love and flood your heart with His glorious presence.

Please be gentle to yourself, my friend. Treat yourself like you would a wounded animal; be patient and kind to yourself. This is the time when you need to be selfish and surround yourself with only those people who will comfort you.

Do only those things you enjoy doing. Postpone unnecessary projects until you have the strength and stamina to tackle them. Be sure to get plenty of rest. Allow yourself ample time to grieve. Do not be in a hurry, but take one day at a time. "Cast all your anxiety on him because he cares for you" (1 Peter 5:7).

As you walk through the wilderness, my friend, you will discover how much the Lord Jesus Christ loves you. He is tenderly watching over you to make sure you are all right.

As you begin to depend on the heavenly Father to provide your *every need*, you will encounter His daily expressions of love. It is in the darkness where you will most see His strong, silent love. You will discover, my dear, He is preparing you for something wonderful, and in a little while, He will replace all of your hurt with His incredible joy!

I love you so much, my cherished friend. I am praying for God's richest blessings on your life.

Hang on to Jesus, my dear. He loves you!
Heather

CHAPTER 5

—⚹—

COMFORT

"Though the mountains be shaken and the hills be removed, yet my unfailing love for you will not be shaken nor my covenant of peace be removed," says the LORD, who has compassion on you.

– Isaiah 54:10

Dearly Beloved:

God loves you so much! He is continually reaching out to you because you are His precious child. He cares for you. He delights in you. He desires to have a wonderful relationship with you, my friend

My former next door neighbor is a very dear friend of mine. She and her family lived across the road from me for years. Three years ago, her husband became sick and one day—in the early spring—he went to be with the Lord.

Several days later, I arrived home late one evening. I drove up the driveway and glanced out the car window toward my neighbor's yard. To my amazement, thousands of fireflies covered the large trees surrounding her lovely home.

The exquisite insects lit up the black night. It seemed like the Lord was telling my grieving friend, "I am here with you. Do not be afraid."

Another evening, two years later, alone in my little house in the woods, I was standing outside in the dark, praising the Lord. It was a summer night and tree frogs were singing loudly to the songs playing on my radio. It was a glorious night; all of creation seemed to be praising God!

Then I noticed hundreds of fireflies penetrating the magnificent night. They were everywhere: in the sky, in the trees, and on the ground. I was overwhelmed with the beauty and majesty of the night.

Dear friend, God loves you. He is there with you to brighten up your dark days and long, lonely nights. He longs to comfort you and give you His precious peace.

Do you know Him, my beloved sister? I pray you do because He will take away the despair in your heart and replace it with incredible joy. If you do not know the One who loves you more than life, please take a minute and ask Jesus into your heart. You will never be sorry.

I love you!
Heather

CHAPTER 6

—ϟ—

PARTIES

Like a lily among thorns is my darling among the young women.

— Song of Solomon 2:2

You are altogether beautiful, my darling; there is no flaw in you.

— Song of Solomon 4:7

Dearly Beloved:

Several years ago, after partying most of a Saturday night, I stumbled into church the next morning with a horrible headache. I felt absolutely awful and thought I was going to be sick. I arrived rather late—church had started several minutes earlier and I could not find a good place to sit.

I have sensitive ears and always sit on the end of the aisle, but today the seats were all filled. I was forced to sit in the middle of a row surrounded by people. In front of me were two small children talking and cutting out paper dolls.

I was hot and miserable. I remember the congregation was standing and singing praises to God when the most incredible thing happened. Suddenly all the irritations vanished, the noise and distractions were gone. My headache went away, and I was ushered into the awesome presence of God.

I cannot begin to tell you what it was like, except His presence was the most wonderful thing I had ever experienced in my life. It lasted until about three o'clock in the afternoon and was so overwhelming I had no desire to eat lunch. All I could do was worship the Father.

When I look back and wonder why the Lord chose that particular moment to appear, I think I know the answer. God knew I desired to draw closer to Him but was still struggling with things that grieved Him. To demonstrate His overwhelming love for me, He picked that exact moment to touch me.

The Father sees your heart, my dear friend. He knows your desire is to please Him. Confess your sins daily to Him, and ask Him to help you walk a life that is pleasing to Him. As you begin to trust in His great love daily, you will experience His wonderful presence in your life. It will enable you to enjoy the good times and bear the hard ones. As we give Jesus more of our lives, He fills us more with His love.

Life becomes a celebration of God's goodness. God bless you, my sister. I am praying for you.

I love you!
Heather

CHAPTER 7

—∽∾—

BUTTERFLIES

My beloved spoke and said to me, "Arise, my darling, my beautiful one, come with me. See! The winter is past; the rains are over and gone. Flowers appear on the earth; the season of singing has come, the cooling of doves is heard in our land. The fig tree forms its early fruit; the blossoming vines spread their fragrance. Arise, come, my darling; my beautiful one, come with me."

— Song of Solomon 2:10-13

Dearly Beloved:

Several years ago I was in a horrible automobile accident that left my beautiful new car smashed and my body filled with pain for months. In the midst of my suffering, the Lord gave me a glimpse of heaven.

One Sunday, following a tremendous church service, I was on my way to Beaverdam to visit my daughter. The ride through the countryside was quite beautiful; sounds and smells of summer were everywhere. Flowers bloomed profusely along the path, cows grazed contently in the pasture, and birds were singing in unison as I drove down the country road.

Struck by the magnificent beauty, I began singing praises to God. In adoration and wonder I exclaimed, "Lord, this is what heaven looks like!"

At that moment I rounded a bend in the road. To my utter amazement—as far as my eyes could see—were millions of tiny golden butterflies. They were everywhere: in the fields, in the air, in the road. I had to dodge to keep from hitting them. They were beautiful.

It seemed like I drove for miles with those exquisite butterflies flooding the countryside. Then I heard a voice deep inside of me say, "Heather, this is what heaven really looks like!"

God bless you, my dear friend. May He continue to thrill your heart with His overwhelming love.

I love you!
Heather

CHAPTER 8

—꽈—

A BROKEN HEART

Why, my soul, are you downcast? Why so disturbed within me? Put your hope in God, for I will yet praise him, my Savior and my God.

– Psalm 42:5

By day the LORD directs his love, at night his song is with me—.

– Psalm 42:8

Dearly Beloved:

God uses so many ways to reach His children: through His beautiful creation, His Word, His voice speaking to our hearts, and people. He sends loved ones to comfort us, inspire us, lift us out of the muck of life, and walk with us through the storms and hard times.

When I lost my husband, God so lovingly provided me with precious friends who loved and looked after me. One sister gave me her bed to sleep in while she slept on the floor, right beside me. Another brought me her slippers and flannel linens to keep me warm. A third met me at work, and we spent our lunch hours in prayer and fellowship.

One sister began praying for me continuously and told her friend about me. Her friend prayed faithfully for four long years. I had heard about her but had never met this beautiful lady until recently at the funeral of a mutual friend. There, in front of the casket, we embraced.

Many other dear friends were there for me. Their love and support encouraged me and helped to keep me going.

My precious family strengthened and comforted me during the difficult months. They loved and walked with me through the valley of sorrow.

One night my beloved son brought me a rose bud and laid it on my bed where I lay crying. My darling daughter ran up her telephone bill month after month to check on me daily; my kind son-in-law never complained. My beloved parents made sure the house was in good repair. My dear mother-in-law and father-in-law loved me.

Many friends came to my rescue. When the furnace room was flooded, leaving the furnace underwater, a good friend spent hours working on it until he got it running. A neighbor dug a deep trench to prevent water from pouring under the house.

Another repaired my dryer and installed a ceiling fan. Still, another neighbor worked on my furnace periodically during the hard winter. One person I never met put in new pipes under the kitchen sink.

Two elders from my church came and visited me the first year. I will never forget what one of them said to me. He said, "Heather, if I lost everything, Jesus Christ would be enough."

Oh, dear friend, God makes a way when all hope is gone. He cares for you, my dear sister, so very much. When you are going through hard times, He is right there. He sees your sorrow. He knows all about it. He understands because He has been there Himself. He has walked in your shoes.

Look to Jesus, my friend. He promised, "Never will I leave you; never will I forsake you" (Hebrews 13:5).

I love you!
Heather

CHAPTER 9

—ɯ—

EXPRESSIONS OF LOVE

See what great love the Father has lavished on us, that
we should be called children of God!

— 1 John 3:1

Dearly Beloved:

God cares for you more than you can fathom. Your every worry and concern is always on His heart. He cares about each minor detail in your life.

Read the wonderful story of Moses and Israelites to see how He tenderly watched over them during the forty years they wandered around in the desert. "Your clothes did not wear out and your feet did not swell" (Deuteronomy 8:4).

He blesses us in other way—with wonderful expression of love. When I first moved to the little house in the woods, the trees were so thick I could not see the stars. I remember one night saying to the Lord, "Father, I can't see the stars."

I thought no more about it until a few days later when I was with my darling prayer partner. She had some gifts for me—one from my Christmas secret pal. I carefully unwrapped the little package; it was a crystal star! So beautiful; I was blown away!

The Father cared about everything that mattered to me. He answered in such a beautiful way. I reverently put it back in the little box and vowed I would keep it always.

Not long ago, I was driving to Virginia Commonwealth University to turn in the final paper for my undergraduate degree in Psychology. I was weary from working on it for several days. It was a chilly afternoon and the parking deck was several blocks from my destination.

I asked the Lord to save a parking space for me in front of the school; however, when I arrived at the university, students were everywhere. It was final examination week, and the school swarmed with students. I thought, *There won't be a parking place for me.*

Turning the corner, I decided to park in an illegal parking space and chance getting a ticket. When I drove around the corner, however, there right in front of the school was a parking place. Just for me!

One Sunday, feeling particularly lonely, I said to God as I got ready for church, "Oh, Father, please let someone invite me to lunch today." After the service, as I was standing by the Christmas card mailbox in the church foyer, a young friend standing next to me asked, "Would you like to have lunch with me today?" We went to the mall and had a marvelous time enjoying our food with each other!

My dear friend, your Father loves you. Tell Him everything that matters to you and then look for His expressions of love!

I love you!
Heather

CHAPTER 10

—∞—

HEAVEN

And we all, who with unveiled faces contemplate the Lord's glory, are being transformed into his image with ever-increasing glory.

– 2 Corinthians 3:18

Dearly Beloved:

Several years ago, God gave me a glimpse of heaven. During a series of events, God began teaching me about how my life is to reflect the radiance of Christ. As I travel the journey of life, I must leave the fragrance of our Blessed Lord along the way. He particularly spoke to me through a T-shirt embroidered with colorful materials and lots of glitter. When I walked, glitter fell off my shirt.

One sunny afternoon in late summer, I was sitting with my prayer partner outside my office under the windmill. We were praying for a dear friend of mine who was going through a difficult time. After the prayer I looked at my prayer partner.

Her face shone with tiny specks of gold, even in her eyelashes! She was the most beautiful creature I had ever seen.

"Oh, Lord," I breathed, "is this what we will look like when we get to heaven?" I knew we would be even more beautiful because we will have brand new bodies like our precious Lord Jesus Christ.

"His face was like the sun shining in all its brilliance" (Revelation 1:16).

"When Christ appears, we shall be like him" (1 John 3:2).

Wow, I can't wait! Heaven will be a place of glorious ecstasy and pure delight. John, the beloved disciple of Christ, described "the Holy City, Jerusalem, coming down out of heaven" (Revelation 21:10). He said "it shone with the glory of God, and its brilliance was like that of a very precious jewel" (Revelation 21:11).

Just thinking about being in that magnificent place with the Lord Jesus Christ thrills my heart! My cherished friend, may God richly bless your life and may His wonderful, glorious presence be with you forever!

I love you!
Heather

CHAPTER 11

—⁓—

THE RAINBOW

Do you not know? Have you not heard? The LORD is the everlasting God, the Creator of the ends of the earth. He will not grow tired or weary, and his understanding no one can fathom. He gives strength to the weary and increases the power of the weak. Even youths grow tired and weary, and young men stumble and fall; but those who hope in the LORD will renew their strength. They will soar on wings like eagles; they will run and not grow weary, they will walk and not be faint.

– Isaiah 40:28-31

Dearly Beloved:

Last fall, while preparing Holy Communion for Sunday morning worship service, I succumbed to a severe flu attack. I was forced to spend the next several days in bed. My doctor took me off all foods for a week!

It was an extremely difficult time because I returned to work long before I was allowed to eat anything. I generally eat all the time; my favorite food is cupcakes. Rarely do I enjoy healthy foods. Perhaps it was why I got so sick.

Anyway, it was hard working day-to-day and consuming only fluids. I became increasingly weak and lost a great deal of weight.

On Thursday, the doctor gave me permission to try a little chicken soup and crackers. *Wow*, I thought, *now I can eat!*

I had hardly taken the first bite when I became deathly sick. So sick in fact, I had no choice but to go home and get back into bed. The doctor instructed me to discontinue eating until the following Monday. Talk about upset!

My faith wavered, and I was discouraged. It is not much fun being sick when you are alone. However, dear friend, I was not alone—the Father was right beside me. I stayed in bed for a couple extra days.

Early Sunday morning, I awakened with my face toward the window. My little house in the woods usually has some sort of wildlife scurrying about. Anxiously, I scanned the trees in vain, looking for something, anything to comfort me—a bird perched on a branch, a squirrel hiding its acorns! However, I received absolutely nothing.

Disheartened, I turned over in the bed and was completely overwhelmed. I could not believe my eyes! For right above my bed was the most beautiful rainbow I had ever seen—in my bedroom! It began at my bedpost, traveled up the wall, across the ceiling, down the wall opposite my bed, and out the door.

Three beams of gold overlapped each other. Yet, each ray was so unique and beautiful itself—the scene was breathtaking!

I laid in bed and stared at the rainbow for twenty or thirty minutes. Then it faded away.

When it disappeared, I got out of the bed and was compelled to prepare Holy Communion. Feeling weak, I got out the grape juice and bread, and spent some time in prayer and fellowship with the Lord. Afterwards, I ate the bread and drank the juice, blessing the precious One who gave His life for me.

It was the first food I had eaten in ten days. It was the beginning of my healing. Praise God! Looking back, it was only fitting for the One who had watched over me so tenderly to be blessed with the first food I ate.

My precious friend, the Father loves you greatly. Please take some time and spend it with Him. He longs to commune with you.

I love you!
Heather

CHAPTER 12

―ᴍ―

SHARING

"For I know the plans I have for you," declares the LORD, "plans to prosper you and not to harm you, plans to give you hope and a future. Then you will call on me and come and pray to me, and I will listen to you. You will seek me and find me when you seek me with all your heart."

– Jeremiah 29:11-13

Dearly Beloved:

Did the Lord ever put in your heart a desire to do something extraordinary, but you had no idea how you would accomplish His plan? You wanted to do this wonderful thing, but you did not even know where to begin.

Listen, my dear friend. When God puts something grand in your heart to bring Him glory, you can be sure He will bring it to pass.

Three years ago during the month of November, the Lord inspired me to decorate the twenty-five foot white pine tree that graced my front yard. This was to be a Christmas gift to my friends and neighbors, thanking them for their love and support over the years. It was to be completed by December 1-the date of the ladies neighborhood Christmas party.

I was thrilled with the idea but was not sure how it would manifest. However, I went to the mall and bought all of the Christmas lights I could possibly afford. I got the little clear lights—hundreds of feet—and lots of extension cords for the big project.

A week before the Christmas party, I took my kitchen chair and the lights and cords, went outside, and sat down by the white pine. I had no idea what to do next. In my garage was a stepladder, but it did not stand much past seven feet and it was pretty wobbly at that.

As I sat in the chair wondering what to do, my prayer partner drove up the driveway. She immediately assessed the situation; she volunteered to go home and bring her long ladder back. It sounded wonderful to me, but I was not sure who was going to climb up the tree.

A few minutes later, she triumphantly returned and brought back with her a friend of her son's who just happened to be at her home. He was an expert at climbing and decorating trees!

My daughter then arrived and she went up the tree with the young man. The two young people spent hours up there, climbing as high as they dared. They patiently wrapped the branches with yards of Christmas lights.

When evening came, we turned on the lights. The scene was breathtaking. Some of the lights blinked and looked like stars twinkling in the sky. News of the tree spread beyond my neighborhood and people drove by to see the wonderful sight. I was blessed most of all!

My dear friend, in sharing your life with others, the hurt and pain you are experiencing will begin to dissipate. Reaching out to other hurting people will bring about a tremendous healing in the very core of your being.

My sister, please reach out to someone less fortunate than you. Caring for another will bring you much comfort and great joy.

I love you!
Heather

CHAPTER 13

—ɷ—

THE CHRISTMAS TREE

Where can I go from your Spirit? Where can I flee from your presence? If I go up to the heavens, you are there; if I make my bed in the depths, you are there. If I rise on the wings of the dawn, if I settle on the far side of the sea, even there your hand will guide me, your right hand will hold me fast.

— Psalm 139:7-10

For you created my inmost being; you knit me together in my mother's womb. I praise you because I am fearfully and wonderfully made;

— Psalm 139:13-14

Dearly Beloved:

What do you do when your heart is broken? When you are discouraged? When you think no one cares? When you cannot go on? What do you do, my friend, to get rid of the pain?

Do you fill up your life with busyness—things that take up your time, but do not comfort your heart? Do you go shopping—spend money you do not have on things you do not need?

Do you camouflage the pain with junk food? Do you go to parties—drink too much and feel awful the next day? Do you get involved with people who are bad for you? Do you take drugs?

My precious friend, these things are only temporary fixes—vain attempts to erase the hurt. They will not heal the grief in your heart. They will not even come close. Beloved, please let me point you to the sure way to alleviate your pain forever.

Several years ago, in early December, I was still grieving over the loss of my husband. My family grieved for me. I was considering checking into a hospital for awhile to try to get well. I knew I needed help in a bad way.

One evening, following a Christmas program at church, I went home sobbing. In desperation, I cried out, "Lord, help me!"

I opened my Bible to the book of Psalms. The Lord comforted me with His precious words. That night, my friend, became the turning point in my life.

I slept soundly for the first time in weeks and awoke the next day feeling different. My first thought was *Christmas is not simply a fun time, but a time to reach out to other hurting people.*

I was not up to giving gifts, but I was able to send Christmas cards to lonely people like myself. God put so many friends in my heart and loved ones who needed a word of hope.

Three days before Christmas, my pastor preached a message that inspired me to buy more cards. I chose a simple design: a lone red cardinal perched on a pine tree. On Christmas Eve, I was still stuffing mailboxes with my messages of cheer.

I did not decorate my home that year. I spent the holidays with my daughter. The house looked as lonely as I felt when I left it on Christmas Eve.

Several days later I returned home and was sitting in front of my picture window. A white pine tree, planted twenty-five years ago by my husband and me, stood proudly in my front yard. It was covered with sparrows.

Suddenly, a bright red cardinal flew over and landed on one of the branches. He stayed awhile, and then flew away. Another cardinal immediately took its place. Christmas music was playing softly on the radio. Then the DJ spoke. He said, "Do not be afraid for you are worth more than many sparrows" (Matthew 10:31).

I was overwhelmed. The Creator of the universe had reached down and given me a Christmas tree; a live one full of His own unique decorations. Nature itself. Just like my Christmas cards!

I wept over His goodness, but that was just the beginning. From that day on, birds of every kind—cardinals, blue birds, sparrows, robins, woodpeckers, and black birds—flocked to my tree. They reminded me of the faithfulness of the Father who tenderly watched over me during my walk through the wilderness. Over the past years, God has used His cardinals to encourage me in a thousand different ways.

My dearest friend, the Father longs to comfort you and take away your pain. "Cast all your anxiety on him because he cares for you" (1 Peter 5:7).

Call out to Him, dear one. He is right beside you.

I love you!
Heather

CHAPTER 14

—⚏—

HOPELESSNESS

I have loved you with an everlasting love; I have drawn you
with unfailing kindness. I will build you up again, and you,
Virgin Israel, will be rebuilt. Again you will take up your
timbrels and go out to dance with the joyful.

— Jeremiah 31:3-4

Dearly Beloved:

Have you ever felt like running away from home?
Have you ever wished there was a quiet spot where you could
go for just a little while to find rest from all of your worries?

I have been in your shoes, my precious friend. I have
searched for a place of comfort or a word of hope and was
bitterly disappointed. When the trials and hard times crashed
down on me, there seemed to be no way of escape.

My dear friends could not comfort me. Even the peace of
God eluded me. He seemed so far away. My prayers did not
appear to go anywhere. I could not feel Him anymore.

In desperation, I realized His Word was my only hope. I began searching the Scriptures for meaning to my overwhelming darkness. Many verses spoke to me, but one profoundly resonated within me.

Consider it pure joy, my [sisters], whenever you face trials of many kinds, because you know that the testing of your faith produces perseverance. Let perseverance finish its work so that you may be mature and complete, not lacking anything. (James 1:2-4)

What a powerful word, my friend. The Lord had not left me. He was there all along, encouraging me to dig deep into His precious Scriptures, to drink deeply of Him. His Word is true, dear one. His Word brings life.

His Word is for you, my sister. I encourage you to spend a few minutes each day in the Holy Scriptures. You will find indescribable riches in His precious Word. Jesus said, "Come to me, all you who are weary and burdened, and I will give you rest" (Matthew 11:28).

This past December I wept over the disappointments in my life and desperately cried out to the Lord for a word from Him. I took my Bible to bed and opened it to read Ezekiel 37:1-14 where it tells of God breathing life into "a great many bones on the floor of the valley, bones that were very dry."[1]

That is the God we serve, dear sister. Nothing is too difficult for Him. He can breathe life into the circumstances that overwhelm us. His Word tells us that "weeping may stay for the night, but rejoicing comes in the morning" (Psalm 30:5).

---

[1] Ezekiel 37:2

Take time tonight, my dear friend, to dig into His precious Word. The Father longs to share His heart with you.

I love you!
Heather

CHAPTER 15

—ᴍ—

GIFTS

Show me your face, let me hear your voice; for your voice
is sweet, and your face is lovely.

— Song of Solomon 2:14

How beautiful you are and how pleasing, my love, with
your delights!

— Song of Solomon 7:6

Dearly Beloved:

God speaks to each of us in different ways. When
we belong to Him, the Lord daily encourages us with His unique
expressions of love. Can you recognize His daily gifts of love
designed solely for you?

For me it is the cardinals. Sometimes He sends them when
I am weary and discouraged. At other times, He is showing His
incredible and awesome love just for me. God makes me feel
like I am the only one in the universe He loves.

When I first moved into my little house in the woods, I drove the long way to work because it was the only way I knew. My son-in-law said I was going ten miles out of the way and told me a shortcut. I apparently missed a turn and five miles down the road, I realized I was lost. I had no idea where I was, but God did.

Just when I was about to give up, I came upon a mailbox with the word CARDINAL written on it. I was amazed! Was that a person's name? I had no idea, but I was encouraged to keep going.

A little while later, I came upon a small weather vane made of wood and cut into the shape of a cardinal. Of course, it was painted bright red! Right beyond the weather vane was the road I had been looking for.

When I went to pick up my college graduation gown for the upcoming ceremony, there was a bright red cardinal in a little tree by the parking deck on the college campus. I knew God was saying, "You made it; I love you, Heather!"

When my prayer partner and I were driving home from church one morning, a red cardinal flew into a puddle of water right in front of us and stopped. We had to slam on the brakes to avoid hitting him.

Once when I was tempted to do something I knew would grieve the Lord, and I had resisted the temptation, a red cardinal hopped through the leaves toward my little house and stopped in front of my window, looking at me. He even waited for me to get the camera and take a picture—twice!

God will do the same for you, my cherished friend. For you are the apple of His eye (*See Psalm 17:8*). You are His most precious creation. He adores you; He loves you so much.

Look for His love for you today, my friend; ask Him to show it to you today the depth of His love for you.

I love you!
Heather

CHAPTER 16

—ɱ—

THE SNOWSTORM

The LORD is righteous in all his ways and faithful in all he does. The LORD is near to all who call on him, to all who call on him in truth. He fulfills the desires of those who fear him; he hears their cry and saves them. The LORD watches over all who love him.

– Psalm 145:17-20

Dearly Beloved:

A few years ago while coming out of my dentist's office, I glanced up at the sky. Across the horizon, big, fluffy clouds were shaped in the form of a cross. *Wow*, I thought, *something wonderful is going to happen.*

I went back to work and forgot about the clouds. When I left the office later in the afternoon, it started snowing hard. The windows of my car were covered and flakes were falling so rapidly, it was hard to get them clean. I did not own a scraper and used my credit card.

It took a while, but I was finally ready to go. I eased out of the parking lot and cautiously merged into the traffic. I did not go too far before I realized the windshield was fogged up; I could not see. The wipers were working, but they did no good. Hurriedly, I rolled the windows down and began to use my hands to clean the window. It did not help—I panicked.

It was pitch dark and the traffic was bumper to bumper. Cars crawled down the highway. Praying for God to do something, I peered through the snow-covered window.

Finally, after what seemed to be hours, we came to a traffic light. I sped through, pulled over at a service station, and got out of the car. I thought, *What is wrong with the defroster?* My bare hands swept away the snow from the windshield and hit something hard. Ice covered the vent. *No wonder I could not see.*

Hastily, I knocked it off, cleaned the window, and got back into the car. In a few minutes, the window was clear, and I took off again. A few minutes later I pulled into the driveway, safe at last. I called my daughter and told her about my adventure.

"Mother," she said, "we are having a blizzard. The weather man is predicting two feet of snow!"

"What?" I cried. "You're kidding! I don't have any food in the house!"

I was really upset with God. I was His beloved daughter. *Why did He not tell me?*

I went to bed and slept fitfully that night. I thought maybe it would stop in a little while, but I did not really believe it.

The next morning I warily peered out my ice-covered windows; it was still snowing. The roads were covered and the flakes were coming down hard. I could barely see and never got out of the driveway. There was no way I could go to the store. I had no idea what to do for groceries.

Oh, dear friend, when we do not know what to do, our Father knows. He loves us and will make a way. We only need to trust Him.

That afternoon, the telephone rang. My friend who lived close by invited me to supper.

"I've made soup, Heather. A big pot, full of everything I could find."

"I don't like soup," I foolishly said. "I'm not coming."

I hung up, and then thought how stupid. My friend was inviting me to supper, and I declined because I did not like the menu!

Hastily, I called back and gratefully accepted her invitation. She had fixed enough soup to last a week. It was a good thing, too, because we could not get out for several days. We ate soup and more soup. It was the most wonderful food I have ever eaten!

God will provide for you, too, my dear. "Cast all your anxiety on Him because He cares for you" (1 Peter 5:7).

I love you!
Heather

CHAPTER 17

—w—

DISCOURAGEMENT

Do not fear, for I have redeemed you; I have summoned you by name; you are mine. When you pass through the waters, I will be with you; and when you pass through the rivers, they will not sweep over you. When you walk through the fire, you will not be burned; the flames will not set you ablaze. For I am the LORD you God, the Holy One of Israel, your Savior.

— Isaiah 43:1-3

Do not be afraid, for I am with you.

— Isaiah 43:5

Dearly Beloved:
      Several years ago, God spoke to me on the way to work. Planning to graduate from college in a few weeks, I was struck down with a debilitating illness that forced me to withdraw from all of my classes. At the same time, I was informed I was going to lose my home.

Devastated over the news, I was also struggling in other areas of my life. Drowning in debt, my faith wavered, and I became discouraged. I knew, however, God had his hand on my life and there was a lesson to be learned. On Tuesday morning, March 23, the Lord showed me.

Driving to work early one morning, my throat ached and I could feel a cold coming on. Most of the night I experienced anxious thoughts and exhaustion wrapped around me like a cloud. Philippians 4:11 came to mind: "I have learned to be content whatever the circumstances."

Then, almost immediately, Romans 8:35-39 flooded my heart: "Who shall separate us from the love of Christ? Shall trouble or hardship or persecution or famine or nakedness or danger or sword? . . . No, in all these things we are more than conquerors through him who loved us. For I am convinced that neither death nor life, neither angels nor demons, neither the present nor the future, nor any powers, neither height nor depth, nor anything else in all creation will be able to separate us from the love of God that is in Christ Jesus our Lord."

Five minutes later, I pulled the car over and wept as His love penetrated and permeated my heart. That is what the Lord wanted me to know—nothing could separate me from Him. Not illness, disappointments, financial hardship, losing my home.

Nothing could separate me from the love of God. He loves me and nothing will ever separate me from Him. The Father loves you, too, my precious friend. Nothing will ever separate you from Him. Hang on to Jesus, dear one. He has His hand on your life.

I love you!
Heather

CHAPTER 18

—ɯ—

LOVER OF YOUR SOUL

For God so loved the world that he gave his one and only
Son, that whoever believes in him shall not perish but have
eternal life.

— John 3:16

Dearly Beloved:
You are treasured by God. You are so dear to Him.
He absolutely adores you. You are His most precious creation.
My sister, the Father cherishes you. You are His beautiful
daughter, His precious child.

The Father longs to have a deep relationship with you, my
dear. He wants to walk with you, talk with you, and listen to your
heart. He wants to share in all of your joys and sorrows.

When you are lonely and discouraged, He is right there
beside you; yearning to comfort and hold you in His strong
arms of love. He, the giver of love, perfect love.

He is always patient, kind, and believes in you. He, my dear friend, is gentle, full of compassion, and eager to encourage and strengthen your heart.

He never disappoints, criticizes, or tears down. When friends let you down, He is there to build you up. When loved ones betray you, He never leaves nor forsakes you.

When the future looks bleak, He lights your way in the darkness. When trials and hard times come, He watches tenderly over you to make sure you are all right.

My precious friend, I pray you know the One who loves you more than life. In this glorious spring season, may the Lord Jesus Christ fill your heart to overflowing with His awesome, incredible, wonderful, marvelous love!

I love you!
Heather

CHAPTER 19

—ɯ—

FOCUS

But God demonstrates his own love for us in this: While we were still sinners, Christ died for us.

– Romans 5:8

Dearly Beloved:

We all need direction in our lives. We need a marker to point the way so we will know if we are on the right track. For many years I was lost and had no idea where I was going. The worst part was I did not know I was lost. It was not until the Father rescued me from the darkness and brought me into the kingdom of His Son when I realized how lost I really was!

It amazes me that the Father loves me. For so many years I walked my own way, totally rejecting Him. Yet, in His great mercy and love, He kept me safe from harm and gently restored me to Himself.

His Son died for me on a cross. That is the marker God keeps ever before me. As long as my eyes are set on the cross, I know I am on the right track.

When I was betrayed and God asked me to extend mercy and grace to those who harmed me, the cross illuminated the sky as I submitted to His will. When people laughed at me during a difficult time, the Father reminded me of His Son dying on the cross while people mocked Him.

When He prompted my heart to apologize to one who offended me and I hesitated, I saw pipes shaped in a sign of the cross at a gasoline station. That afternoon I asked for the person's forgiveness.

When I carried a heavy ladder to clean a window for one who had hurt me, He reminded me of Christ carrying His cross for me. When I am weary and discouraged, I see the cross in the clouds in the sky.

My dear friend, Jesus died on the cross for you. Keep your eyes fixed on the cross. Then you will know you are on the right track!

I love you!
Heather

CHAPTER 20

—ɱ—

DREAMS

May he give you the desire of your heart and make all your plans succeed.

— Psalm 20:4

Dearly Beloved:

The words of the psalmist, which read: "Take delight in the LORD, and he will give you the desires of your heart" (Psalm 37:4) have always been a favorite of mine. For years I had a dream to go to graduate school, but it had always seemed impossible. After all, I had just turned fifty-one, approximately thirty years too late. Besides, I needed to pass a horrific examination and obtain three recommendations—at least one from a college professor.

Going to school at night did not provide much of an opportunity to establish a relationship with the instructor. However, my friend, with God nothing is impossible!

Two years ago, I planned to graduate from college with a bachelor of science degree. I had pursued the degree for years and hoped to finally put it to rest. Just a few weeks before the big day, I came down with a severe case of bronchitis. I got behind in my assignments and was forced to drop all of my classes. I was extremely upset.

Could not God have kept me well for just a little while longer? I could not imagine why He, who had made provision for me to go to school, would suddenly deny me of the joy of finally reaching my goal.

However, my cherished friend, our timetable is not necessarily His. God sees into the future. He was not saying no to my plans, but not yet. Only He knew why. I was not told until much later.

In the fall of that year, one of the classes I was required to take met at a time of day when I was unable to attend. This meant a further delay in graduating. Again I could not understand God's reasoning for not letting me graduate.

Oh, my friend, if only we could fully trust the One who loves us "because anyone who comes to him must believe that he exists and that he rewards those who earnestly seek him" (Hebrews 11:6).

My scheduled date to graduate was delayed until August. I had to take my final class that summer, missing the spring commencement exercises. When I walked into Psychology 406, a young college professor greeted me. The class was full and I was late, but he was kind.

The class was challenging and fun, but extremely difficult. The professor supplied extra materials for us to study, which helped to make sense of the complex information. His encouragement helped to reduce my anxiety on the study of sensory perception.

Several weeks later, I was attending a Fourth of July celebration at my church. Everyone was outside eating ice cream, and I stood in line talking to the people behind me. Suddenly, right in front of me, was my college professor.

My mouth fell open; I could not believe my eyes—my professor was at my church! I had been going to school for years and knew only a few Christian professors. To have one attend my church was a miracle.

We talked a few minutes and I spoke of my concern over his class. He then said something I will never forget. My professor said, "Heather, I will pray for you."

My friend, can you believe it? My professor was going to pray for me. I went home and fell on my face before the Lord and wept over His goodness.

I got to know Professor Kelley and his beautiful wife, Cindy, over the next months. He was planning to obtain His doctorate the following year; the same time I would participate in the ceremonies.

Over the Christmas holidays, after much prayer and serious thought, I decided to apply for graduate school. My friend, the program I applied to was uniquely tailored for me. It required no examination and the third recommendation I needed, God so beautifully supplied. It was Dr. Brian Kelley!

My friend, if I had graduated on the original date, I would not have had Dr. Kelley as my professor. My final class was the first class he taught independently.

My dear sister, the Father loves you immensely. Delight in Him and He will give you the desires of *your* heart.

I love you!
Heather

CHAPTER 21

—⚮—

FEAR

The LORD himself goes before you and will be with you;
he will never leave you nor forsake you. Do not be afraid;
do not be discouraged.

– Deuteronomy 31:8

And surely I am with you always, to the very end of the
age.

– Matthew 28:20

D early Beloved:
It is time to move again! Some people like to move
once in a while. It gives them a chance to clean out clutter that
seems to fill up a house so quickly. It offers people a fresh start,
a new beginning. New challenges wait to be conquered.

Not for me. Moving is hard. I cannot bear to part with the
memories of a lifetime. So, I take them with me. I find it hard

to uproot and begin again. I like security and feeling safe in my own little world.

When I lost my home of thirty years, I could not believe it. How could God allow this to happen to me: His daughter, His child? Where was my Father when I needed Him? I though He loved me.

Angrily, I lashed out at Him. Bitterly, I shouted at the One who gave His life for me. My friend, I deeply grieved my precious Lord. I broke His heart.

But, dear one, we serve a God full of compassion and mercy. He forgave me, but He had His way.

The Lord took me off to a little house in the woods and began a work deep in my heart. During this time of solitude:

He has given me a passionate love for Christ.

He has given me a deep love for humanity.

He has given me a hunger for His Word.

He has given me compassion for the lost.

He has filled my heart with incredible joy.

More importantly, He has taught me to trust Him completely with my life. Now, He is calling me to move again. It is still hard, but this time I trust the One who goes before me. As long as He is holding my hand, I am not afraid.

My dearest friend, do not fear when God calls you to pick up and start again. You are His chosen: His beloved, His bride. He will tenderly watch over you and provide for all your needs. Hold tightly to Jesus, my sister. He loves you!

Heather

CHAPTER 22

—ɯ—

LOVE

Let him kiss me with the kisses of his mouth—for your love is more delightful than wine.

– Song of Solomon 1:2

How beautiful you are, my darling! Oh, how beautiful!

– Song of Solomon 4:1

How delightful is your love, my sister, my bride! How much more pleasing is your love than wine, and the fragrance of your perfume more than any spice!

– Song of Solomon 4:10

My dearest friend:

You are deeply loved by God; you are dear to Him. He absolutely adores you. You are His most precious creation. My sister, the Father cherishes you. You are His beautiful daughter!

You are His beloved. The Father longs to have a deep relationship with you, my dear. He wants to walk with you, talk with you, and listen to your heart. He wants to share in all of your joys and sorrows.

My friend, the Father yearns to share His heart with you. He has so many wonderful things to tell you; things for your ears alone. Listen. Can you hear Him? Christ is gently knocking at the door of your heart. Please invite Him in, today.

Please tell Him you love Him and want to serve Him. Tell Him you are sorry for your sins and desire for Him to wash and cleanse you with His precious blood.

My friend, He will give you a brand new life. The Lord has so many glorious adventures in store for you, my dear sister. When you and God are walking together, you will experience His love in wonderful ways. Your prayers to the Father will bring Him much pleasure; He will flood your heart with indescribable joy.

You will daily encounter His marvelous expressions of love; unique ways only you will recognize. Your devotion to Jesus will grow stronger each day. Your intimate times with Him will be glorious ecstasy and pure delight. You will be filled with the power of the Holy Spirit to touch the lives of others with compassion, mercy, and grace.

My precious friend, may our glorious God and Savior pour out His blessings on your life and may He surround you each second of the day with His awesome, magnificent, powerful, wonderful presence.

I love you!
Heather